Sovereignty of God

Is God Really in Control?

A Short Read

by

Chris **Cree**

SOVEREIGNTY OF GOD: Is God Really In Control?

Published by SuccessCREEations, LLC

To all those who are disillusioned, frustrated, or confused by the contradiction of a loving God whom you've been taught is causing so much pain in our world.

And especially to those who are about to give up on God altogether because of this apparent contradiction.

God is so much more wonderful than you know. He truly is a good, good Father. As you renew your mind to His goodness you will begin to experience an intimacy with Him that will completely transform you so powerfully it will impact the world around you too.

CONTENTS

Introduction

Why This Book?

This idea that *God is in control*, often referred to as the *sovereignty of God*, is one of those theological ideas that causes some significant challenges in the lives of believers. Believing God controls everything that happens kills intimacy with God, causes confusion, and creates a victimhood mindset in followers of Jesus. We'll talk about each of these later in this book.

The idea that "God is in control" seems like it honors God because many mistakenly think that absolute control over everything at every moment is a fundamental requirement for God to be God. In fact, it's not unusual for theologians to state something along this line of thinking as if it's a self-evident truth.

That's wrong on both accounts. It's neither self-evident, nor true. Even though God is indeed all knowing (omniscient), and all powerful (omnipotent), there is no reason why God *must* be in control of everything in order to be God. It turns out the truth of God's sovereignty is in no way contradicted, or even diminished, by His choice not to control everything that happens to mankind. We'll unpack this more too.

It can be comforting to believe God is sovereignly controlling everything that happens for a couple of reasons. For some, it shifts responsibility for the things they do and don't do onto God, along with the consequences of those choices.

Others find it comforting to think that God is controlling events when something horrible happens which is completely outside of their own control. Life happens. And some people find comfort in the idea that God meant for them to suffer in order to serve some greater purpose of His.

Unfortunately it's a false comfort because God is not in control of everything that happens here on planet Earth. The Bible is very clear on this issue, as we will soon see.

We will also look at one of the major consequences of this unbiblical view of the sovereignty of God in believer's lives. We'll explore a huge contradiction this theology creates. And we'll close out this short read with some personal insights from my own life.

A great many Christians believe God really does control everything that happens here on earth. There was a very popular Christian song when I first became a believer all about how God is in control.

I sang that song with gusto along with everyone else because that is how God was explained to me as a new Christian. It wasn't until years later that I dug into the scriptures to search out this topic for myself. I guess I kind of just accepted what I was told by the leaders of the various churches I belonged to. After all, they had theology degrees and I didn't.

Imagine my surprise when I discovered that God really isn't controlling everything today. It shook my world. My studies changed my perspective and exposed major problems this misunderstanding of God's nature caused for me.

Yet it also liberated me at the same time. Now I'm free to have a far more intimate relationship with my Father in heaven. Not only that, but gaining a right understanding in this area empowered me to become far more fruitful and effective at pushing back the darkness and partnering with God to expand His Kingdom here on earth.

I want you to have the opportunity to experience this same freedom and blessing in Christ.

This is why I originally pulled the core of this material together for an article on our NewCREEations Ministries website. I regularly receive requests for that article in a print version for people to use in Bible studies and whatnot.

This short read format book is my way of honoring those requests.

Now let's get started!

Chapter 1

Power vs. Authority

Misunderstanding Scripture

People who say God is sovereign, and by that mean He is in control and directly responsible for everything that happens in our world, misunderstand a couple things that are explained in scripture.

One of the things I notice in conversations with people who hold this view, is that their opinion is almost never anchored in what is actually written in the Bible. Typically it comes out in simplistic generalized statements, the most common of which is simply, "of course God is in control."

Again, I think it goes back to the basic misunderstanding that absolute control is a fundamental requirement for God to be God. A great many people just assume this must be the case without ever truly digging into the Bible to see what scripture has to say on the topic.

It's critical that we learn what the Bible actually says. Otherwise we may very likely get things wrong.

The scary part is sometimes people who make it their life's work to pore over the scriptures completely miss huge things that are there in the Bible ready to be revealed to them.

We know this can happen because of what Jesus said to some religious leaders who came to question Him on a matter of the Law,

> *Jesus answered and said to them, "You are mistaken, not knowing the Scriptures nor the power of God."* — Matthew 22:29

If even those who are well versed in scripture can get something so wrong during the earthly ministry of Jesus, then it's certainly possible that even highly trained theologians might have it wrong on this point today.

I'm not so arrogant to ignore the possibility that I might be wrong myself. My desire is for the truth, even when I find that requires me to completely adjust my understanding of something. And that's exactly what happened for me with this. When I dug into scripture I realized I had it wrong. So I adjusted my thinking accordingly.

The reality is that there are folks who do reference scripture by mostly taking a verse or two out of context, which they use to support their predetermined understanding of God's nature. But that's backwards. We don't look for passages in the Bible to "prove" our viewpoints. Instead we should look at the whole counsel of scripture and adjust our views to match that truth.

That said, let's dig into what the Bible has to say on this topic.

Power vs. Authority

When it comes to the question of God's sovereignty and whether He controls everything, the first thing we need to understand is the difference between power and authority. God is indeed all powerful. One of the many names of God is El Shaddai, which means Lord God Almighty.

However, even though God is all powerful, He sovereignly chose to self-limit His power by delegating authority to mankind in the Garden of Eden,

> *Then God said, "Let Us make man in Our image, according to Our likeness; **let them have dominion** over the fish of the sea, over the birds of the air, and over the cattle, over all the earth and over every creeping thing that creeps on the earth." So God created man in His own image; in the image of God He created him; male and female He created them. Then God blessed them, and God said to them, "Be fruitful and multiply; fill the earth and subdue it; **have dominion over** the fish of the sea, over the birds of the air, and over every living thing that moves on the earth." — Genesis 1:26-28*

As you see in that passage, God gave Adam and Eve dominion over "all the earth." With that delegation of authority, God made man responsible for what happens here on earth. It also meant that God could only intervene when there was agreement with mankind because of God's own sovereignly self-imposed limitation of authority.

Because God said mankind has dominion, if He then stepped in the earth to do stuff uninvited, God would be violating His own word. That is something God cannot do (Psalms 89:34).

God of This World

Of course Adam promptly sinned and thereby abdicated his authority to Satan who then became the god of this world. The New Testament tells us that Satan gained this authority on the earth,

> *If the Good News we preach is hidden behind a veil, it is hidden only from people who are perishing. **Satan, who is the god of this world**, has blinded the minds of those who don't believe. They are unable to see the glorious light of the Good News. They don't understand this message about the glory of Christ, who is the exact likeness of God. — 2 Corinthians 4:3-4*

Later, God made covenants with different people. First was Noah (Genesis 9:8-17), and then Abraham (Genesis chapters 15 and 17). Obviously there was the Old Covenant with the nation of Israel, which gave us the Law. These covenants gave God the "legal" right to intervene in specific ways with specific people.

One of the many characteristics of God is that of justice, as the Bible reveals,

> *Therefore the Lord will wait, that He may be gracious to you;*
> *And therefore He will be exalted, that He may have mercy on you.*
> **For the Lord is a God of justice;**
> *Blessed are all those who wait for Him.* — Isaiah 30:18

> *He is the Rock, His work is perfect;*
> **For all His ways are justice,**
> *A God of truth and without injustice;*
> *Righteous and upright is He.* — Deuteronomy 32:4

Because justice is part of God's nature, He does not just arbitrarily do stuff. God is the one who put Adam in charge. Once God did that, He couldn't just arbitrarily take that authority back from Satan just because Adam abdicated it to him.

Fortunately for mankind, God had a way to restore our authority perfectly in keeping with His just nature.

Authority Given to Believers

In the fullness of time, along came Jesus. He lived a truly righteous life, fulfilled the Law, and took all authority back from Satan,

> *And Jesus came and spoke to them, saying, "All authority has been given to Me in heaven and on earth.* — Matthew 28:18

Jesus then delegated that authority to us, His New Covenant believing followers. Here are some examples, starting with the next verse in Matthew,

> *Go therefore and make disciples of all the nations, baptizing them in the name of the Father and of the Son and of the Holy Spirit, teaching them to observe all things that I have commanded you; and lo, I am with you always, even to the end of the age." Amen.* — Matthew 28:19-20

7

> *Then He called His twelve disciples together and gave them power and authority over all demons, and to cure diseases.* — Luke 9:1

> *And He said to them, "I saw Satan fall like lightning from heaven. Behold, I give you the authority to trample on serpents and scorpions, and over all the power of the enemy, and nothing shall by any means hurt you.* — Luke 10:18-19

> *As You sent Me into the world, I also have sent them into the world.* — John 17:18

Jesus also gave us the keys of the Kingdom of Heaven,

> *And I will give you the keys of the kingdom of heaven, and whatever you bind on earth will be bound in heaven, and whatever you loose on earth will be loosed in heaven.* — Matthew 16:19

Now the authority over the earth resides in us as believers. This means we have the authority to do far more than most Christians are doing on the earth today. Unfortunately very few Christians believe they have any real authority. Instead they are mostly standing around waiting for God to do stuff that He has already assigned and empowered us to do, often because they think "God is in control."

God Does Not Approve Satan's Activity

We should take a moment to talk about the stuff Satan does here on earth. One variation of the sovereignty of God teaches that, *OK. God doesn't do everything Himself. But God does have approval authority over everything that happens.*

This view tries to split the difference by claiming that God is still in control even though He doesn't do the bad things Himself. People in this camp say God appoints Satan to do the bad stuff and Satan can only do the bad stuff that God allows him to do.

These folks point to Job as the primary source for this. But they misunderstand what's happening in this passage,

> *So Satan answered the Lord and said, "Does Job fear God for nothing? Have You not made a hedge around him, around his*

household, and around all that he has on every side? You have blessed the work of his hands, and his possessions have increased in the land. But now, stretch out Your hand and touch all that he has, and he will surely curse You to Your face!"

And the Lord said to Satan, "Behold, all that he has is in your power; only do not lay a hand on his person."

So Satan went out from the presence of the Lord. — Job 1:9-12

Satan isn't getting approval from God to mess with Job there. Instead Satan basically pointed out that God was protecting Job "illegally" because He didn't have the authority to do so. Satan was the god of this world because of Adam's sin.

Therefore, by protecting Job, God was encroaching on Satan's authority on earth.

Importance of Covenants

Later, God established covenants with various people. Those covenants gave God the legal right to bless those who were part of the covenant.

As we saw above, justice is part of God's character (eg. Deuteronomy 32:4, Isaiah 30:18). Therefore God must have a legal means to bless people in order for Him to be just and stay true to His own nature. Covenants are that legal means.

The New Covenant with Jesus is the mechanism through which God's authority and power flow as we bring the Kingdom of God to the world around us. It is vital that we as believers and followers of Jesus understand covenants today and the difference between covenants and contracts.

With a contract, if one agreeing party does something in violation of the contract then it is considered broken. The whole contract becomes null and void. Basically the signers of a contract agree to hold up their ends as long as the other signatories hold up theirs too.

With a covenant, both parties agree to hold up their ends regardless of whether the other party keeps their part of the agreement. A violation of a covenant by one party doesn't matter as far as the other party's responsibility to continue to do what they agreed to do.

Covenants are becoming increasingly rare in our culture today. Most folks only think in terms of contracts. Therefore it is important for us to teach the difference between these two arrangements.

Otherwise we hold a faulty view of our relationship with God.

We naturally filter everything we understand about God in terms of a contract. We assume that if we don't hold up our end then, contractually, God won't hold up His. As a result we find it impossible to approach a Holy God because we know we can never hold up our end of the bargain. The standard is perfection and we know we're not perfect.

Of course organized religion would have us believe that it is a contract. Far too many religious leaders use fear of punishment to try and keep us in line. They talk about how we must "get right with God" and keep us focused on everything we do wrong. They paint a picture of a God with a big stick just waiting to whack us when we get out of line.

Who in their right mind would want to relate to a God like that?

Fortunately the truth is that we relate to God in the framework of a covenant. God has already committed to treat us in light of Jesus' perfection even when, *especially* when, we don't measure up. Now it's up to us to choose to believe this truth.

Losing sight of God's covenant with us and framing our relationship with God in terms of a contract completely warps our understanding of who God is and how He thinks of us. And it completely ties us down so that we never come close to meeting our full potential.

God's Original Plan

This brings us back to the original order of things that God put in place as we see in Psalms, for example,

What is man that You are mindful of him,
And the son of man that You visit him?
For You have made him a little lower than the angels,
And You have crowned him with glory and honor.
You have made him to have dominion over the works of Your hands;
You have put all things under his feet — Psalms 8:4-6

We could preach a whole sermon series from that passage. But now I want to focus in on that word that both the KJV and the NKJV translate as "angels" in verse five. That word is translated over 2500 times in the KJV Bible as "God" and only once, here in this passage, as "angels."

Look at how the New Living Translation renders that passage,

What are mere mortals that you should think about them,
human beings that you should care for them?
Yet you made them only a little lower than God
and crowned them with glory and honor.
You gave them charge of everything you made,
putting all things under their authority — Psalms 8:4-6 (NLT)

This accurately describes our position in Christ. We are a little lower than God (but above the angels believe it or not!) We have been put in charge of everything God made. We have been given authority over "all things" according to that passage.

That is a sobering truth because we have been given a huge responsibility here in this life.

Unfortunately we tend to be woefully inept at exercising that authority. For many, a huge part of that ineptness is that they are waiting for God to do things that He has already authorized them to do themselves.

Most Christians have no idea they have been given any authority. No one has ever shared this truth with them. People can't have faith for something they've never heard about!

Chapter 2

Multiple Forces at Work

Additional Forces Working on Earth

Another big thing people who misunderstand sovereignty get wrong is that they have this sense that God is the only force at work in our world today. However, even though he is already defeated, Satan is still operating today and steps in wherever believers fail to exercise their God given authority,

> *Whose minds the god of this age has blinded, who do not believe, lest the light of the gospel of the glory of Christ, who is the image of God, should shine on them.* — 2 Corinthians 4:4

As believers it is our responsibility to shine the light in every dark place to displace the power of the enemy. Again, most Christians live in fear of Satan, not realizing they have been given authority over him in Christ.

When we fail to exercise our authority, Satan is happy to take over.

In addition we have more than seven billion people on the planet who all have individual wills of their own and often do stupid things.

Then on top of all that creation itself has been subject to corruption compliments of Adam's fall,

> *For the creation was subjected to futility, not willingly, but because of Him who subjected it in hope; because the creation itself also will be delivered from the bondage of corruption into the glorious liberty of the children of God.. —* Romans 8:20-21

Starting at least as far back as the time of Noah the planet has been unstable with earthquakes, floods, hurricanes, tornadoes, fires, mudslides, tsunamis, etc. All of these things bring death and destruction to millions. We know that God does not send these things because He instead brings life and peace,

> *My covenant was with him, one of life and peace,*
> *And I gave them to him that he might fear Me;*
> *So he feared Me*
> *And was reverent before My name. —* Malachi 2:5

Since those natural disasters bring neither life nor peace, they cannot be from God.

So there are therefore a whole host of other forces acting in this world which are responsible for the bad stuff. As we've seen here, the Bible is very clear on this.

God Not Author of Bad Things

God is not the author of the bad things that happen in our world, regardless of misguided theology that claims He is,

> *Do not be deceived, my beloved brethren. Every good gift and every perfect gift is from above, and comes down from the Father of lights, with whom there is no variation or shadow of turning. —* James 1:16-17

The simple truth is, God does not cause calamity today. Many people get turned around on this for a number of reasons.

For example a lot of folks look at Romans 8:28 which says,

> *And we know that all things work together for good to those who love God, to those who are the called according to His purpose.*

Many people look at that and say, "See! God brought this on me to do good things with it. He gave me this cancer so that He would be glorified"

Wrong, *wrong* and **wrong!**

Yes, God is with you through the cancer. Yes, He will bring good from it and will be glorified as you draw closer to Him in your trial. God will take that lemon and make lemonade out of it.

But God did NOT bring it on you.

God is in the business of taking the lemons life hands us and making sweet lemonade out of them. He's not in the business of handing out lemons.

Did you ever notice how very often there are police officers around when there is a traffic accident?

It's sort of like how God is always present when bad things are happening to us.

Yet if we were to say that because police are at the scenes of so many accidents then they must be the ones who cause them, we'd be fools.

Unfortunately, that's exactly what people say about God. "God's there in my trial so it must be His fault."

I could go on and talk about how we only ever see Jesus healing people in the Bible. He never put sickness on anyone, not even once. But there are many instances when Jesus healed everyone present.

I could also talk about how Jesus was cursed so that we could be blessed. In this New Covenant age we have a very different arrangement with God than they did in the Old Testament.

But the point is this. God is not causing any of the bad things that happen in our world today.

Our Choice

Even in the Old Testament, under the Old Covenant, people were presented with a choice,

> *I call heaven and earth as witnesses today against you, that I have set before you life and death, blessing and cursing; therefore choose life, that both you and your descendants may live;* — Deuteronomy 30:19

It's like God gave them a pop quiz. *"OK, you've got two choices: life and death. Or you could say it's blessing and cursing. Which are you going to choose?"*

Fortunately God has so much grace that He immediately tells them which is the right answer: *choose life!*

I like tests where the teacher gives the answer!

Every day in a thousand little ways we make choices that either add life to a situation or bring death to it. The life choices bring blessing. The death choices bring cursing into our lives and the lives of those around us.

What we are doing with all these choices is putting the universal law of sowing and reaping into action. The Bible says it this way,

> *Do not be deceived, God is not mocked; for whatever a man sows, that he will also reap.* — Galatians 6:7

Our vertical relationship with God works on the principles of grace and faith. At the same time, everything on the horizontal level here on earth works on the principles of sowing and reaping.

We are free agents in respect to being able to make choices about whom we serve. Unfortunately a great many Christians are not sowing much good seed. Therefore they rarely harvest much either.

It's a life test that we all have before us day in and day out. Those choices are ours alone. We have the ability to choose. Fortunately if any are unsure which answer is right for this test, remember God tells us the right one. Choose life.

If people had a choice back then, that meant God was not controlling them. Believers are also offered a choice today too,

> *Therefore submit to God. Resist the devil and he will flee from you.*
> — James 4:7

Submitting to God and resisting the devil is a choice. Otherwise James would not have told us to do it.

Unfortunately, far too many Christians today have it upside down. They are submitting to the devil and resisting God. But that's a whole big topic for another time.

God's Will Clearly Thwarted

If the sovereignty of God doctrine was true and God really was in control of everything, then it would be impossible for anything to happen that goes against God's will, right?

Yet scripture contains at least one very clear example of God's will being thwarted. In his second letter Peter is talking about how God is patient and outside of time. Then he makes this statement,

> *The Lord is not slack concerning His promise, as some count slackness, but is longsuffering toward us, not willing that any should perish but that all should come to repentance.* — 2 Peter 3:9

God is not willing that anyone should perish. Universalists point to this passage as evidence that everyone is ultimately destined for Heaven. But that cannot be what Peter meant there because that view conflicts with other passages of scripture. The Bible clearly says that many will not end up in Heaven.

For example, Jesus said that many will ultimately find destruction,

> *Enter by the narrow gate; for wide is the gate and broad is the way that leads to destruction, and there are many who go in by it. Because narrow is the gate and difficult is the way which leads to life, and there are few who find it.* — Matthew 7:13-14

Right there Jesus said "many" will follow the road that leads to destruction. "Many" is far more than "not any." You can look it up.

Then we find this in Revelation,

> *But the cowardly, unbelieving, abominable, murderers, sexually immoral, sorcerers, idolaters, and all liars shall have their part in the lake which burns with fire and brimstone, which is the second death.* — Revelation 21:8

Again, that scripture clearly states that at least some (in reality many) people will perish and be destroyed. This is true even though Peter said it's not God's will for anyone to perish.

So clearly God's will does not always come to pass. Therefore God cannot be in control of everything and that "sovereignty of God" doctrine which claims He is must be false.

Chapter 3
What About Job?

Facts Are Not the Same as Truth

To keep things confusing, there are some passages in Job that seem to indicate that God is indeed in control of everything all the time. We already addressed one of those passages in Chapter one.

It's important for us to look at Job in its proper context. We need to keep in mind that the Bible is true, but every word in the Bible is not necessarily *truth*. For example, the Bible accurately records conversations. Those conversations truly happened. But sometimes ungodly people are the ones talking and they say things that are untrue.

We're talking about the difference between facts and truth. The Bible accurately records facts, even when those facts convey untruths.

We see an example of this in Numbers where the Bible records words spoken by those with Korah who rebelled against Moses and Aaron. This is what it says,

> They gathered together against Moses and Aaron, and said to them, "You take too much upon yourselves, for all the congregation is holy, every one of them, and the Lord is among them. Why then do you

exalt yourselves above the assembly of the Lord?" — Numbers 16:3

The Bible accurately records what those wicked men said. But what they said was not true about Moses and Aaron. We see a similar thing with Job.

The Book of Job basically divides into three sections. The first two chapters are introduction where we see a conversation between Satan and God and Job loses everything. Next we have 36 chapters of conversation between Job and his friends. Then, finally in chapter 38 God joins the conversation and speaks for four chapters.

God basically rebukes everyone. Then Job repents, prays for his friends, and gets his prior fortune restored double at the end of the book.

This is what Job says in the last chapter of the book,

> *I have uttered what I did not understand,*
> *Things too wonderful for me, which I did not know.* — Job 42:3b

Job flat out says that he didn't know what he was talking about. Therefore we cannot base our theology on the things he said such as, "The Lord gives, and the Lord takes away. Blessed be the name of the Lord."

When Job said that he was talking like a fool. He later admitted so himself. Therefore, it is foolish of us to build our understanding of God on such statements of his.

Then, right after Job admits he didn't know what he was talking about, God gives this rebuke to Job's friends,

> *And so it was, after the Lord had spoken these words to Job, that the Lord said to Eliphaz the Temanite, "My wrath is aroused against you and your two friends, for you have not spoken of Me what is right, as My servant Job has."* — Job 42:7

Job repented and said what was right, specifically that he didn't know what he was talking about. However Job's friends didn't repent and therefore were further rebuked by God. God said that the things Job's friends said about God were not true.

Therefore we should not look to those passages quoting the things either Job or his friends said to get insight into God's nature and character.

Following Job or Jesus?

Job seems to be one of the favorite books of the Bible for those most passionate about defending an extreme view of the sovereignty of God and idea that God is in control of everything. He is the one they seem to want to model their lives after.

But that's the wrong model. We should be looking to Jesus instead. After all, Jesus is the author and finisher of our faith,

> *Therefore we also, since we are surrounded by so great a cloud of witnesses, let us lay aside every weight, and the sin which so easily ensnares us, and let us run with endurance the race that is set before us,* **looking unto Jesus**, *the author and finisher of our faith, who for the joy that was set before Him endured the cross, despising the shame, and has sat down at the right hand of the throne of God.* — Hebrews 12:1-2

We should be looking to Jesus, who is the perfect example for us, not Job. We are in Christ and are called Christians, not "Jobians."

We should be growing so much like Jesus that we can legitimately say to others, *"imitate me, just as I also imitate Christ"* (1 Corinthians 11:1).

Unfortunately, if you were to say something that bold in most Christian circles today you would be seen as arrogant by most, and probably as heretical by many. But we're called to disciple others and mentoring is the best way to make disciples by far.

Those who look to Job as their model of what it means to be a child of God will be very poor disciples of Christ.

I suspect this sovereignty of God theology that elevates Job to nearly the same status as Jesus is one of the main reasons why so much of Christianity is so ineffective today. It's much like Paul's warning to

Timothy about those who have a form of godliness, but denying its power. Paul goes on to instruct Timothy to keep away from such people! (2 Timothy 3:5).

How Things End

Speaking of following Jesus, Paul shares a bit about how things will ultimately end in his first letter to the Corinthians. In the last chapter of that book Paul reveals how Jesus is the firstfruits of those raised from the dead. He says that we will all be raised up with Him.

Then Paul says this,

> *Then comes the end, when He delivers the kingdom to God the Father, when He puts an end to all rule and all authority and power.*
> — 1 Corinthians 15:24

According to that verse there is a time coming in the future when Jesus will put an end to all rule, authority, and power. Therefore it stands to reason that those things must still exist now.

And if there is power and authority that exists now which will be put to an end in the future, that means God cannot be the only power and authority operating today.

If God is the only force working on the earth today, then that would necessarily mean Jesus has already put an end to all other authorities and power. However, that can't be the case because Paul is obviously talking about things in that chapter which are still off in the future.

For example,

> *Behold, I tell you a mystery: We shall not all sleep, but we shall all be changed— in a moment, in the twinkling of an eye, at the last trumpet. For the trumpet will sound, and the dead will be raised incorruptible, and we shall be changed.* — 1 Corinthians 15:51-52

History hasn't heard *that* trumpet sound yet. Therefore the time when Jesus puts and end to all authority hasn't yet happened either.

And that means those other authorities, rulers, and powers are still out there operating in our world today.

But praise God their days are numbered!

Chapter 4

Victimhood and Other Problems

Sovereignty of God Is Not Absolute Control

As we can see, the Bible is very clear that God is not in absolute control of everything that happens today.

Please understand. God is indeed sovereign. However, the sovereignty of God does not mean what many people think it means.

God is indeed paramount and supreme in the universe. If that's what we mean when we talk about the sovereignty of God, then we are correct. Even so, by now it should be clear that there are other forces at work on earth today.

Some people reject that because they feel it somehow diminishes God. But it doesn't.

Acknowledging the truth that other forces besides God are at work in our world doesn't take any glory away from God. Quite the contrary. The fact that God is still accomplishing His purposes which He planned before the foundation of the world, even without being in control of everyone and everything, reveals God to be even more glorious.

This lines up with what Job said about God towards the end of that book when acknowledging he didn't what he was talking about earlier,

> *I know that You can do everything,*
> *And that no purpose of Yours can be withheld from You.* — Job 42:2

People who claim God controls everything that happens in our world often quote that verse. However, it does not say God controls everything. Instead it simply acknowledges that every purpose of God will ultimately come to pass. God bringing His purposes into fruition even with all these other forces at work today is an amazing testimony of His goodness and glory.

Unfortunately a great many prominent preachers today hold to the erroneous view about the sovereignty of God, believing God is, in fact, in control of everything. Not only that, but we have entire denominations within Christianity that hold to this view.

That so many hold to this view is especially unfortunate because of the problems it creates for the folks who see God this way.

Sovereignty of God Creates Distance

One of the major consequences of this extreme sovereignty of God theology is that it creates distance between Father God and His children. Seeing God as the author of pain and destruction prevents true intimacy with Him.

Who can trust someone they believe probably will send some disease or disaster our way at any time just to teach a lesson?

It is just about impossible to have any true intimacy with someone you think might potentially cause you harm. You'll aways have your guard up. There is an ever present tension and anxiety hanging there just below the surface.

This lack of intimacy perverts our understanding of love.

Apart from God it is impossible to truly know what love is. As God's people lose a clear experiential understanding of God's kind of love because of their lack of intimacy with Him, lawlessness increases. This in turn causes the love of many to grow cold,

> *And because lawlessness will abound, the love of many will grow cold.* — Matthew 24:12

Christians who say that God is in control of everything are accusing God of doing all sorts of horrible things. At the same time, they obviously see that these same things are criminal when they done by a human being.

That doesn't make any sense.

When Jesus was talking about prayer and intimacy with the Father, He said it this way,

> *"You parents—if your children ask for a loaf of bread, do you give them a stone instead? Or if they ask for a fish, do you give them a snake? Of course not! So if you sinful people know how to give good gifts to your children, how much more will your heavenly Father give good gifts to those who ask him."* — Matthew 7:9-11 (NLT)

There Jesus says that God is far better than sinful people. But too many Christians flip that on its head. They make God far worse than sinful people by saying He is responsible for horrible evils that happen in our world.

You cannot be truly intimate with someone you expect is likely to deliberately cause you pain at any moment.

Sovereignty of God Creates Confusion

This extreme sovereignty of God view that says God controls everything all the time makes for some convoluted theology. In their attempts to reconcile the conflict created from the mistaken understanding that a loving God is also responsible for horrible suffering and disasters, theologians invented different concepts like God's sovereign will, His permissive will, and His perfect will.

Really what they are doing is trying to bury the obvious paradox with enough intellectual sounding words that people will accept it. It's like if they blow enough smoke, people won't realize there is no substance behind it.

Think about it for a moment.

How is God glorified by putting sickness on someone?

And if we really did believe that sickness was from God, why in the world do we go to doctors or take medicine to try and get better? Shouldn't our going to the doctor be futile because we're attempting to go against the will of God by getting better?

It makes no sense because it turns good and evil upside down. We are unwise at best when we do that,

> *Woe to those who call evil good, and good evil;*
> *Who put darkness for light, and light for darkness;*
> *Who put bitter for sweet, and sweet for bitter!* — Isaiah 5:20

In the Bible the word "woe" indicates doom and pending judgement. Isaiah is saying that those who call evil good and good evil are setting themselves up for some really bad stuff.

Therefore it creates confusion when believers muddle good and evil by claiming God is responsible for evil.

Sickness is always portrayed in the Bible as a curse. To pretend it is somehow a blessing is a perversion that misrepresents the Kingdom of God.

Not only that, but it's obvious people don't really believe God is in control. If they truly thought God put whatever sickness on them, then they wouldn't be taking so much medicine or going to the doctor.

Their actions contradict their theology.

Sovereignty of God Creates Victims

Another problem we see in the body of Christ is that people who think that God controls everything see themselves as helpless victims. If God actually caused whatever bad thing is happening, that means the only way to get God's help in that situation is to convince Him to change His mind.

The challenge there is the numerous verses in the Bible that address God's unchanging nature. Here's one example,

> *God is not a man, so he does not lie.*
> *He is not human, so he does not change his mind.*
> *Has he ever spoken and failed to act?*
> *Has he ever promised and not carried it through?* — Numbers 23:19 (NLT)

Since changing God's mind seems effectively impossible to most Christians, they typically resort to begging and pleading with God. But those prayers are ineffective because they are filled with doubt.

James tells us that's the exact wrong way to ask for anything from God,

> *For let not that man suppose that he will receive anything from the Lord; he is a double-minded man, unstable in all his ways.* — James 1:7-8

Jesus said the way for us to see our prayers answered is to believe and not doubt,

> *For assuredly, I say to you, whoever says to this mountain, 'Be removed and be cast into the sea,' and does not doubt in his heart, but believes that those things he says will be done, he will have whatever he says. Therefore I say to you, whatever things you ask when you pray, believe that you receive them, and you will have them.* — Mark 11:23-24

But how can you believe God will heal you and make you well when you also believe that He is the one responsible for you being sick in the first place?

This faulty theology creates a situation overloaded with doubt at a time when the person praying desperately needs to be free from all doubt.

When people are dominated and controlled by others, they live afraid of what bad thing might happen next. Over time, that terror eats away at their souls and creates a powerlessness that comes with being constantly victimized by things outside their control.

This victimhood mindset is completely at odds with the powerful overcomers the Bible says we now are as children of God in Christ,

> *For whatever is born of God overcomes the world. And this is the victory that has overcome the world—our faith.* — 1 John 5:4

Our true identity is that of an overcomer, not a victim. Until we stop blaming God for the bad stuff that happens in our world and realize that God has equipped us with authority and power to deal with much that is wrong, we will never walk in that true overcoming identity that is ours by right of inheritance.

But you don't even have to look at the bad things which happen to know that God is not controlling everything or everyone. We can simply consider God's most prominent characteristic.

Which brings us to the next chapter.

Chapter 5

Identity Problem

Control is Unloving

Here's a radical statement. Control is in opposition to love.

John tells us that God is love,

> *He who does not love does not know God, for **God is love**.* — 1 John 4:8

> *And we have known and believed the love that God has for us. **God is love**, and he who abides in love abides in God, and God in him.* — 1 John 4:16

Then Paul gave us an excellent definition love,

> *Love suffers long and is kind; love does not envy; love does not parade itself, is not puffed up; does not behave rudely, does not seek its own, is not provoked, thinks no evil; does not rejoice in iniquity, but rejoices in the truth; bears all things, believes all things, hopes all things, endures all things. Love never fails.* — 1 Corinthians 13:4-8

Do you notice anything about that passage?

Nowhere in that explanation of what love looks like do you see love described as controlling, manipulative, afflicting, humiliating, or deceptive.

Did you know that there is a god that does have attributes? This is how Muslim scriptures describe Allah.

That's something to think about.

However, according to that definition in 1 Corinthians above, love does not control others, plain and simple. Therefore, if the God of the Bible is love, then He cannot be controlling everyone or everything.

Most people can easily see that a parent who attempts to control every aspect of their adult children's lives is fostering an unhealthy relationship. Yet that's exactly how some view God, as a totally controlling father.

To paraphrase Jesus, if you can see good parenting in earthly fathers, how much better must your Father in heaven be?

Slaves Instead of Sons

One big area where this whole extreme "God is in control" sovereignty of God messes people up is with the understanding of their identity. We touched on this in the last chapter. But it even goes beyond the victim mentality to where people actually take on a slave mentality without even realizing it. This slave thinking affects everything they try to do in life.

Here are some characteristics of a slave mindset.

Slaves Have Masters — Slaves have no autonomy. They are property so they have no freedom to choose what they do. They must do what their masters tell them, or they will suffer the consequences.

Slaves Have No Rights — Because they are property, slaves don't have the rights that citizens have. They are a lower class and completely subject to the will of their master.

Slaves Do Only What Are Told — Slaves don't take initiative because they don't know their master's business. Therefore they can't anticipate their master's wishes. When slaves finishes a task they stop and wait for the next thing they are told to do. For the slave, doing nothing is far better than doing the wrong thing. Slaves also don't ask "why?" It doesn't matter if what they are told to do makes no sense to them. They don't get to question it.

Slaves Fear Punishment — Because slaves are property and considered lower class people, they live in fear of punishment for their mistakes. This is their primary motivation for doing good work.

Slaves Are Poor — Slaves are given just enough by their masters to complete their assignments and survive. Because a slave is the property of their master, they cannot really own anything. Everything the slave has is owned by their master anyway.

Now let me ask you. Does that not sound like how a great many Christians view their relationship with God?

Some of you reading this may think that's exactly how we are supposed to relate to God.

If so, I get where you are coming from. But here's the problem. We were born into slavery. In Adam, we were slaves to sin. Slavery is all we knew.

Because slavery is all they know, many just shift their slavery status from being a slave to sin over to being a slave to God. And you can even find scriptures that seem to support this view.

But what if I told you God intends a much different relationship with you?

Father God has adopted you into His very own family as one of His children,

> *For as many as are led by the Spirit of God, these are sons of God. For you did not receive the spirit of bondage again to fear, but you received the Spirit of adoption by whom we cry out, "Abba, Father."*
> — Romans 8:14-16

That is truly incredible. You have been adopted into God's own family, not as a slave, but as a son!

I should take a moment to address a cultural issue here. Far from excluding women in this, Paul actually elevates women by using the term "sons." Let me explain.

First, we know Paul means both men and women when he says that we are sons of God because of what he says in this passage here,

> *For you are all sons of God through faith in Christ Jesus. For as many of you as were baptized into Christ have put on Christ. There is neither Jew nor Greek, there is neither slave nor free, there is neither male nor female; for you are all one in Christ Jesus.* —
> Galatians 3:26-28

When Paul says, "there is neither male nor female," he is not making a statement about biology. Paul is not denying that humans come in both male and female form. Instead, it's an emphatic statement that there are no class considerations when it comes to believers. Where the Kingdom of God is concerned, there is no longer any distinction between Jews and non-Jews, between slaves or free people, nor between men and women. Once we are in Christ, each of us now has the exact same direct access to God through Jesus as every other believer.

We also all have the same potential for authority in the Body of Christ, regardless of whether we are male or female. So those who think that women cannot be leaders in the Kingdom of God are completely off base.

I know it's counterintuitive. But really Paul was elevating the status of women considerably by calling us all "sons of God." In the culture at the time, women were effectively second class citizens. For example, in Paul's day women were not allowed to be taught by rabbis.

Jesus thoroughly upended that cultural restriction because we see numerous times where women such as Mary learned at the feet of Jesus.

Also, inheritance was passed down through the male heirs. So, if Paul had said, "sons and daughters" in that culture and that time, it would have meant he was talking about two different classes of people.

By inspiring Paul to say we, "are all sons of God," the Holy Spirit elevated women in the Kingdom of God to a co-equal status with men. I could write a rather lengthy book on the whole topic of how Jesus and the New Testament views women.

But my point is this:

When we see "sons of God" in the New Testament, it means "sons *and daughters* of God" the way we understand it today in our culture.

So, if you're a woman know this. Jesus values you every bit as much as us men. You are every bit as capable of being a leader in the Kingdom of God as men are.

Now let's take a moment to think about how sons see the world.

Sons have Fathers (vs. slaves have masters) — There are all kinds of fathers out there, just like there are all kinds of masters out there. In both cases, some are better than others. But at its core, the primary difference between the two is that the father/son relationship has love at its core, and the slave/master relationship has expediency as its foundation.

Sons are Family (vs slaves have no rights) — Family brings a significantly increased amount of liberty. For example, your children have much more liberty to access things in your house than the neighbor kids do. Plus, your kids have a lot more right to ask things of you as their parent. You will do things for your own child that you would never consider doing for someone else's kid.

Sons have Autonomy (vs slaves only do what are told) — As our children mature, we give them more and more autonomy to make their own choices. We do everything for a newborn baby. But by the time our teenager gets their driver's license, they have earned a much higher level of trust to be allowed to make many of their own choices. (Hopefully anyway.) But most of us will be a lot less willing to give our car keys to someone else's teenager.

Sons are Loved (vs slaves fear punishment) — Fathers love their children. Even horrible fathers often do what they do because they have a desire for the best for their children. They just have a twisted view of what love means. Fortunately our Father in Heaven understands love better than anyone. There is no fear of punishment as we come to understand His love.

Sons Receive Inheritance (vs slaves are poor) — Fathers pass on their legacies through their children. That means the question "why?" is very important to children. The reason behind what they are instructed to do can often be even more important than the task itself. That's why Jesus said,

> *No longer do I call you servants, for a servant does not know what his master is doing; but I have called you friends, for all things that I heard from My Father I have made known to you.* — John 15:15

It's also why Paul told us we are joint heirs with Christ,

> *The Spirit Himself bears witness with our spirit that we are children of God, and if children, then heirs—**heirs of God and joint heirs with Christ**, if indeed we suffer with Him, that we may also be glorified together.* — Romans 8:16-17

You are not just family. You are an heir with Jesus to God's entire Kingdom!

When we come to understand that far from controlling our every action like a slave, God is instead looking to engage with us in a truly loving and beneficial Father/son relationship, it changes everything. God truly longs to include you in on what He's doing in the world. You are His precious child. Don't be afraid to ask Him what's up!

Chapter 6

What About Romans 9?

The Challenge

We must acknowledge that there are a great many very intelligent theologians who look at the same Bible and come away believing that God is indeed in control. They get there because there are a few passages in the Bible that do appear to indicate that God arbitrarily dictates what happens in our own lives here on earth.

Then they use the understanding they took from these few isolated passages as a filter to get their understanding of everything else in scripture.

Romans chapter nine is one of these key passages.

On the face of it Romans nine seems to be saying that God is indeed in control of everything that happens in the course of history. There Paul talks about how God loved Jacob but hated Esau. He says that God hardened the heart of Pharaoh. And He uses the example of the potter's clay which cannot tell the potter how to fashion it.

They use this chapter together with the three passages where Paul uses the word "predestined" in his writings as the basis for their doctrine that God controls everything that happens. Here are those references,

> *For whom He foreknew, He also predestined to be conformed to the image of His Son, that He might be the firstborn among many brethren. Moreover whom He predestined, these He also called; whom He called, these He also justified; and whom He justified, these He also glorified..* — Romans 8:29-30

> *having predestined us to adoption as sons by Jesus Christ to Himself, according to the good pleasure of His will,* — Ephesians 1:5

> *In Him also we have obtained an inheritance, being predestined according to the purpose of Him who works all things according to the counsel of His will,* — Ephesians 1:11

These three passages, combined with Romans chapter nine form the foundation for the sovereignty of God theology that a huge number of Christians believe today.

It is a compelling case. At first glance they do indeed appear to say that God predetermines everything that happens in our world. I believed that way for many years. So I understand where folks are coming from with that perspective.

However, when I studied the issue out for myself, beyond the surface scriptures, I arrived at a very different conclusion.

Please keep in mind that it is not my intention to write an exhaustive theological treatise here. I'm simply sharing my perspective why I no longer believe the Bible teaches that God controls everything that happens in our lives.

That said, let's dive in.

Context Matters

It is vital to consider the context when examining a passage of scripture. The Bible combines thoughts and ideas to make larger points. We get a much clearer, more accurate understanding of what is being said in a particular verse or passage when we take into account the greater context around that portion of scripture.

Context makes all the difference when we look at Romans chapter nine.

Here Paul is talking about God's master plan of salvation. The larger point he makes is that God, in His sovereignty, has the right to choose how He is going to bring salvation to the world.

In the course of making this greater point, Paul reviews Israel's past in Romans nine. As he does so, Paul establishes how God operated through a promise instead of either through direct lineage or through obedience to the Law.

Remember, the Jews of Paul's day considered themselves to be God's chosen people because they descended from Abraham, Isaac, and Jacob, and because they followed the Law. Paul is making the case here in Romans that God has always operated through promises and that His true people are actually those who receive His promises by faith.

After reviewing Israel's past in Romans nine, Paul goes on to talk about Israel's present in Romans ten. Then he continues on to talk about Israel's future in Romans eleven.

The whole thing starts with Abraham believing a promise, that through him God would bless the entire world. Earlier in Romans Paul said that Abraham believed God, and God counted it to him as righteousness (Romans 4:3). Paul says that we receive the blessing the same way, by believing God's promise

This passage reveals the point of what Paul is getting at in Romans nine,

> *But it is not that the word of God has taken no effect. For they are not all Israel who are of Israel, nor are they all children because they are the seed of Abraham; but, "In Isaac your seed shall be called." That is, those who are the children of the flesh, these are not the children of God; but the children of the promise are counted as the seed.* — Romans 9:6-8

Paul says that it is those who believe the promise of God who are the rightful heirs of Abraham, not those who are descended from him, nor those who obey the Law.

The rest of the chapter is devoted to proving this point. To do so, Paul starts with Jacob.

Jacob was the child of promise even though Esau was the first born and should have received the blessing in the natural. Paul highlights this by quoting from Malachi about God loving Jacob but hating Esau.

His point is not that God arbitrarily chose one over the other. Instead Paul is saying that God sovereignly chose to carry the blessing on to the one who believed the promise instead of to the one who was next in line in the lineage.

If you remember the story, Jacob put so much value on both the birthright and his father's blessing that he schemed his way into getting both of them. Jacob believed in their value far more than Esau. For example, look at what Genesis has to say about the birthright,

> Then Jacob said, "Swear to me as of this day."
>
> So he swore to him, and sold his birthright to Jacob. And Jacob gave Esau bread and stew of lentils; then he ate and drank, arose, and went his way. Thus Esau despised his birthright. — Genesis 25:33-34

Esau despised the birthright that was his so much that he traded it away for a light lunch of stew and bread. Jacob had a different view. He valued it so much that he took advantage of an opportunity to trade it for something his brother wanted to feed his own flesh.

Jacob had tons of issues. But he did value the things of God. Esau had at least as many character flaws. On top of those flaws he also despised the things of God. Their priorities affected their destinies.

Pharaoh's Heart

Ultimately God has the right to determine how He will show mercy.

We see this again with the case of Pharaoh. We must go back and look at what the scriptures say about his heart and bring that information forward into Romans chapter nine for clarity as we look at Paul's comment about God hardening his heart.

When we read through the Exodus account with an eye to see exactly what happens to Pharaoh's heart, we discover a clear pattern of progression.

First we see that Pharaoh's heart grows hard,

> And **Pharaoh's heart grew hard**, *and he did not heed them, as the Lord had said.* — Exodus 7:13

> *Then the magicians of Egypt did so with their enchantments; and* **Pharaoh's heart grew hard**, *and he did not heed them, as the Lord had said.* — Exodus 7:22

Next we see Pharaoh hardening his own heart,

> *But when Pharaoh saw that there was relief,* **he hardened his heart** *and did not heed them, as the Lord had said.* — Exodus 8:15

> *But* **Pharaoh hardened his heart** *at this time also; neither would he let the people go.* — Exodus 8:32

Only then, after we plainly see Pharaoh clearly depicted as hardening his own heart more than once, do we see Exodus say that God hardened Pharaoh's heart,

> *But* **the Lord hardened the heart of Pharaoh**; *and he did not heed them, just as the Lord had spoken to Moses.* — Exodus 9:12

Based on this sequence of events we see that Pharaoh was not a robot simply following a program that God forced upon him. Instead, God knew what was already in Pharaoh's heart and how he would respond to the situation. God used what He knew Pharaoh would do to both bless the people of Israel and to bring glory to Himself in the process.

We see that God knew how Pharaoh would respond elsewhere in scripture. For example,

You showed signs and wonders against Pharaoh,
Against all his servants,
And against all the people of his land.
For You knew that they acted proudly against them.
So You made a name for Yourself, as it is this day. — Nehemiah 9:10

Really what was going on there is that God responded to Pharaoh in the same way that God responds to anyone who determines in their heart to practice ungodliness.

We see this in Romans chapter one. Paul describes people who do a whole bunch of ungodly stuff starting in verse 18. Then in verse 24 he says, *"Therefore God also gave them up to uncleanness, in the lusts of their hearts."*

Those people filled their hearts with ungodliness first, then God responded by giving them up to even more ungodliness. Then the cycle repeats as Paul goes on to say this,

And even as they did not like to retain God in their knowledge, God gave them over to a debased mind, to do those things which are not fitting; — Romans 1:28

Again, as with Pharaoh, it's a case of God responding to what people do in their own hearts. God is not a cruel sadistic programmer in the sky churning out people who robotically do ungodly stuff. Instead, He responds to what is in our hearts. God won't be a part of the bad things people do. Instead, He gives them over to the unclean debased mind that they desire so much.

The Potter's Wheel

We have a great deal of input into what kind of vessel God will make of us. Paul makes this clear in his instructions to Timothy,

But in a great house there are not only vessels of gold and silver, but also of wood and clay, some for honor and some for dishonor. Therefore if anyone cleanses himself from the latter, he will be a vessel for honor, sanctified and useful for the Master, prepared for every

good work. Flee also youthful lusts; but pursue righteousness, faith, love, peace with those who call on the Lord out of a pure heart. But avoid foolish and ignorant disputes, knowing that they generate strife. And a servant of the Lord must not quarrel but be gentle to all, able to teach, patient, — 2 Timothy 2:20-24

That passage puts a condition on what type of vessel the individual becomes: "if anyone cleanses himself". It doesn't say that God arbitrarily decides what type of vessel we will be and there is nothing we can do about it.

Like Jacob and Esau, we each have some personal responsibility when it comes to reaching our destiny.

Not only is this true of us individually, but it is also true of nations as well. If we go to the prophetic imagery of the potter in Jeremiah chapter eighteen that Paul refers to in Romans chapter nine we see this to be true.

There, the prophet sees a potter working a lump of clay on the wheel. He started moulding the clay in one direction, but when the clay became marred, the potter fashioned the lump of clay into something else.

This is what God says is the lesson of the potter's wheel,

> *if that nation against whom I have spoken turns from its evil, I will relent of the disaster that I thought to bring upon it. And the instant I speak concerning a nation and concerning a kingdom, to build and to plant it, if it does evil in My sight so that it does not obey My voice, then I will relent concerning the good with which I said I would benefit it.* — Jeremiah 18:8-10

There God says He has the ability to change the direction of a nation if and when the nation chooses the path of good over the path of evil. Once again, God sovereignly exercises His ability to shape a destiny in response to the choices people make.

God doesn't say His point to the potter's wheel illustration is that He arbitrarily shapes nations on a whim.

Those Predestination Verses

As you can see, Romans chapter nine is not really saying that God is completely controlling everything that happens on the earth. Instead, God sovereignly chooses to work with people, and even in response to what is in their hearts, as He brings about His plans and purposes for humanity.

In this light, let's take another look at those verses which contain the word "predestined" and see what they mean.

First we have the passage from Romans chapter eight,

> *For whom He foreknew, He also predestined to be conformed to the image of His Son, that He might be the firstborn among many brethren. Moreover whom He predestined, these He also called; whom He called, these He also justified; and whom He justified, these He also glorified.* — Romans 8:29-30

God is all-knowing. Because He resides in eternity outside of time, God sees the end from the beginning. That means God knows how we will respond to Him. God "foreknew" those who will receive Him.

But knowing that something will happen is *not* the same thing as causing it to happen.

That passage clearly says that God knew in advance that some would choose Jesus; and once they did, He then predestined them to be conformed to the likeness of Jesus. God doesn't arbitrarily destine some people to heaven and others to hell.

Next let's look at Ephesians 1:5. That verse occurs right in the middle of a thought. So this time let's include the verses immediately before and after it,

> *just as He chose us in Him before the foundation of the world, that we should be holy and without blame before Him in love, having predestined us to adoption as sons by Jesus Christ to Himself, according to the good pleasure of His will, to the praise of the glory of His grace, by which He made us accepted in the Beloved.* — Ephesians 1:4-6

When we look at the additional verses we see it says that God sovereignly decided that those who are in Christ should be holy and without blame and and adopted as sons. It says God chose those of us who are in Christ to become these things, not that God chose to arbitrarily put some of us in Christ.

It's now the destiny for those in Christ which God has predestined, not whether or not individuals are in Christ. Once people believe in Jesus, God predetermines the outcome of their choice.

People get to choose Jesus or reject Him. Once they do that, God predestines the outcome of their choice. We are free to choose. But the consequences of our choice are already set by God.

Then with the other instance of the word predestined, we also need to add some context to get a full understanding,

> In Him also we have obtained an inheritance, being predestined according to the purpose of Him who works all things according to the counsel of His will, that we who first trusted in Christ should be to the praise of His glory. — Ephesians 1:11-12

This passage says that we, "who first trusted in Christ" are predestined to "be to the praise of His glory." Again, it does not say that God predestines who will accept Jesus and who won't.

God has not predetermined who is saved and who is lost. Instead, God has predetermined the destiny of those who willingly believe and also the destiny of those who willingly reject His gracious gift of righteousness,

> that is, that God was in Christ reconciling the world to Himself, not imputing their trespasses to them, and has committed to us the word of reconciliation. Now then, we are ambassadors for Christ, as though God were pleading through us: we implore you on Christ's behalf, be reconciled to God. For He made Him who knew no sin to be sin for us, that we might become the righteousness of God in Him. — 2 Corinthians 5:19-21

As Paul says in the passage above, God has done His part. Now, Paul says, "we implore you to be reconciled to God."

Statements like this from Paul urging folks to turn to God only make sense when we understand that God has not predetermined who will choose Him and who will reject Him.

So you can see, a strong Biblical case can be made that Romans chapter nine is not talking about God being in control of everything. And when we consider all the other evidence, I think the case is airtight.

Now let's move on into the personal and the practical.

Chapter 7
Personal Experience

My Own Personal Challenges

I know this sovereignty of God theology creates problems for a great many Christians because I experienced it first hand.

Before I became a believer I generally was able to accomplish whatever I set my mind to do. Once I decided I would do a thing, it pretty much always happened.

As just one example of this, when I was in the navy I got my first choice of assignments across the board. I was selected for aviation over ships and submarines. I wanted to fly jets, not helicopters or propeller planes. Not only that, but I got the specific type of jet I wanted. Then I got the duty station I wanted. And finally, I even was assigned to my first choice squadron.

The navy always prioritizes its needs over the desires of the individual. Even so, I always seemed to get my first choice anyway. And it wasn't because I was some sort of over achiever, the top of my class, or the best at doing much of anything. Instead I was very much average, somewhere in the middle of my class.

Looking back, that's just how my life worked in those days. Often I didn't have strong preferences and generally took whatever came my way. But most any time I really did care and decided on a thing, it just seemed to happen.

The first thing I encountered in my life that I couldn't "just decide" to do was quit drinking. I was a drunk. No matter what I tried to do, I kept drinking. Ultimately my inability to overcome alcohol on my own is what let me to Jesus. He gloriously set me free from that bondage.

However, I met Jesus through folks with an extreme understanding when it came to the sovereignty of God. They taught me God is in control of everything. These well meaning folks told me that God made me a drunk so that He would be glorified by my deliverance.

That created a huge problem in my Christian walk. I experienced first hand how horribly traumatizing alcoholism was in my life. I saw how it messed with every part of my life, from my relationships, to my finances, and even into my health.

Anyone who would deliberately subject me to that kind of pain and suffering was not someone I could be intimate with. This meant I had an unhealthy view of God right out of the blocks in my Christian walk. My relationship with Him suffered as a result.

My response makes sense. As I said in Chapter four, you won't have an intimate relationship with someone you believe might cause you harm at any moment. You will have your guard up.

It is impossible to be truly intimate and guarded at the same time.

Sovereignty and God's Will

Lining up with the will of God was one of the huge challenges I faced in my early days as a believer. I was taught that blessing was found when our lives were lined up with the will of God and problems came our way when we drifted outside God's will for our lives.

Like the slave in the previous chapter, I quickly came to understand that doing nothing was better than doing the wrong thing. As a result, I became a powerless victim to whatever "God willed." I may not have been walking in the blessings of God that I saw on the pages of scripture. But I was free from my alcohol addiction, which truly was a tremendous blessing. Beyond that, at least I wasn't being punished for being outside of the will of God.

When you think about it, this creates a logical contradiction.

If God is in control of everything, then everything that happens must be in His will. That would mean no matter what we did, we could never be outside His will. And if we're always in the will of God, then we should always be blessed and bad things shouldn't ever happen to believers, right?

But you only need to spend about ten minutes on Facebook to see all sorts of bad things happening to Christians.

Since I was taught that God truly is in control of everything, then it sure seemed to me that He is abusive because apparently it's His will that lots of bad things happen to His people. Yet the Bible says that God is perfectly loving and not abusive.

It all made for a jumbled, confusing understanding of God because the God I saw on the pages of scripture didn't line up with the God I was taught was true. And my practical experience was still different yet from those two views of God.

The result of all that confusion about God's will is that I was what I call, "saved and stuck." I was absolutely certain that I would be in heaven once I stepped into eternity.

But here and now? My life was a hot mess.

I put up a good front, mind you. All the while inside I was a fearful, frustrated ball of confusion. Life seemed heavy and hard, the complete opposite of the light burden and easy yoke Jesus said He puts on us.

The Bible says that the Kingdom of God is righteousness, peace, and joy (Romans 14:17). That certainly wasn't my experience back then. For example, Lisa and I had trouble communicating, which meant we argued a lot. That was just one of a great many things in my life that didn't line up with what I saw on the pages of scripture.

And it never seemed to improve.

Because I had no real intimacy with the Father, I had no idea what His will really was for my life. I was just really sure I didn't want to be outside of whatever that will was because I was told that's when bad things happened.

Fortunately, as I renewed my mind to the truth of God's sovereignty, that He didn't create me to be a drunk, and that He's not causing all the bad stuff in this world, then I was able to finally experience intimacy with my Father in heaven.

As that intimacy grew, God did reveal His will for Lisa and me. He invited us to join Him in what He is doing in Scotland. Imagine our surprise at being asked, *"Do you want to?"* Such a kind, gentle question asking us what we wanted to do was radically different from the stern, controlling God I was taught about before.

We can argue theology all day long. But our understanding of God should have a postive, practical effect in our lives. Otherwise it's just pointless religion.

Jesus told us to look at fruit our lives produce (Matthew 7:20). Applying that standard to my own life confirms to me I now have a far better understanding of these scriptures than before.

Then, I was passive, expecting God to do whatever needed doing, yet rarely ever experiencing Him move in my life. I could only point to my own prayers being answered in the vaguest sense, which others could easily attribute to coincidence. Beyond my salvation and being set free from the bondage of alcohol, there was nothing supernatural in my own life I could point others to as evidence God was real.

Now, with my current understanding of these scriptures and God's nature, I experience Him moving in my life constantly. Lisa and I often see God answering our prayers so specifically that it effectively eliminates random chance as the explanation. And we pray far more boldly as a result.

With the understanding that Jesus delegated His authority to us as believers (Matthew 28:18-20), and that Jesus promised we would do the things He did (John 14:12), experiencing the supernatural has become our new normal. Now my life is full of peace and joy, where before there was very little of either.

Then, I bounced around from job to job looking for the next big thing to bring some significance and meaning to my life. Now Lisa and I live overseas, partnered in a specific assignment we personally received directly from God to make disciples, expand the influence of His Kingdom, and impact nations.

When I consider the fruit produced in my life by these two views of God, there's no comparison. God is no respecter of persons. You can see the same increase in fruitfulness too by adjusting your perspective of God in this area.

Please understand. Experience is not the source of truth. Truth is found in Christ as laid out in scripture. Experience can, however, be useful to confirm truth, which is why Jesus told us the importance of fruit.

Fight, Freeze, or Flee

From what I've observed, the contradictions and lack of intimacy wrapped up in this extreme sovereignty of God theology cause one of three reactions in Christians.

In my case, I froze and became a powerless victim. I didn't want to make any wrong decisions and get outside God's will. At the same time I had no intimacy with Him to truly find His will. Besides, I thought that God's will was going to come to pass regardless of what I did.

As a result, I froze. I tried to put up a good appearance of confidence. In truth, the foundation where my faith was trying to anchor was a shaky mess of contradictions and lack of intimacy with God.

I see the same quiet desperation in the lives of many other Christians.

Looking back, that was a radical departure from my generally confident, hard charging approach to life prior to believing in Jesus.

Personally, I think this is a big reason why so many ungodly people tend to accomplish so much more than the typical Christian. Many believers are frozen, unwilling to take risks because they are afraid of stepping outside God's will. This strong aversion to taking risks prevents them from reaping great rewards.

Meanwhile, unbelievers don't have the same shackles on when it comes to taking risks.

A second way I see some Christians respond to the these contradictions is with belligerence. Instead of freezing they pick a theological fight with anyone who dares to acknowledge the contradictions to their view that God is in control of everything. Those folks are not fun to be around because they tend to go off on abusive rants against those who disagree with them.

Their behavior makes sense. If they think God's character is abusive because He is responsible for all the bad things happening in the world, why would they behave any differently?

They're easy to find on social media because they tend to be some of the most argumentative. Take an informal survey when you encounter particularly rude or obnoxious Christians by asking them, "Is God in control?"

I suspect the overwhelming majority of the time they will respond with a yes.

The other response I've seen in folks with this view of the sovereignty of God which says God is in control of everything is perhaps the saddest. They simply walk away from Christianity altogether.

They rightly see the contradictions of this this theology. Because they can't reconcile a loving God with all the suffering He is accused of causing in our world, they reject Jesus and look for answers elsewhere.

Then to compound the tragedy, often their "God is in control" believing friends mostly write them off as "not predestined" to follow Jesus.

It's enough to make a person want to scream.

The Truth Will Set You Free

These responses are why I say this theology is so insidious. None of those responses produces the powerful, overcoming, world changing, royal priesthood of believers we see on the pages of the New Testament. Instead we see powerless victims waiting for God to do stuff that He's told us to do.

Many like to quote Ephesians 3:20 that says God is able to do immeasurably more than we can ask or imagine. But they gloss over the last part of that verse. He does these things according to the power that *works within us*. It's not all God and none of us. Nor is it all us and none of Him. It's God working *through* us. When His power is combined with our agreement it can accomplish impossible, miraculous things in our world.

This is good news. God is not in control of everything! There are other forces at work in our world today.

That means we can trust God's character to always want the very best for us. The door for intimacy with the Father is wide open!

Then we can truly taste and see that the Lord is good. The more we experience God's goodness, the more we want to experience it. Over time we really can become more intimate with God.

Intimacy is vital because the God wants to partner with you to accomplish His purposes on the Earth by pushing back the darkness and advancing His Kingdom here, now, today. The world needs more believers who live in the powerful place of intimacy.

We live in dark times. The need for powerful world changers to rise up in the Church has never been greater than it is today.

God is inviting you to join Him. The first step is to stop blaming Him for all the bad stuff that happens.

About the Author

Chris Cree was a merchant marine officer and flew off of aircraft carriers in jets with the US Navy. After leaving the Navy he spent 12 years working on the docks in various marine cargo operations positions. In 2007 Chris turned his blogging hobby into a new career developing websites, both in his own business as a freelancer and as an employee of a rapidly growing firm. This job change provided the flexibility to eventually leave the coast where the ships were, move to the mountains and go to Bible college.

Chris and his wife Lisa founded NewCREEations Ministries in 2013 as a vehicle to answer God's call on their lives to guide believers into their full inheritance in the Kingdom of God. They live in Scotland as missionaries, where they lead a local campus of an international Bible college.

You can learn more and contact them with questions or other inquiries via their NewCREEations.org website.

Also by Chris Cree

Rejecting Mammon: How to See Results From Your Giving

Church Websites: How to Communicate the Gospel Effectively in a Social Media World

Made in the USA
Middletown, DE
20 January 2020

83476483R00035